SOCIAL SAUNA

BATHING
&
WELLBEING

A moment of stillness in the sauna ritual, Mikkeli, Finland, 2010. Image © Alexander Lembke

SOCIAL SAUNA
BATHING & WELLBEING

Jane Withers & Ria Hawthorn

Jane Withers
Studio

THERMEGROUP

Löyly Design Sauna by Avanto Architects, Helsinki, Finland, 2016. Image © Kuvio.com

CONTENTS

Dr Robert C. Hanea,
Founder and Chairman of Therme Group

At Therme Group, we have an open and collaborative philosophy, exploring future-focused concepts through the lens of human and environmental wellbeing. We believe the world's problems can only be solved through an interdisciplinary approach. Our wide-ranging interests include subjects such as art, architecture, botanics, cities, engineering, psychology, society and much more. In exploring these varied disciplines, including through our programmes such as Therme Art, we aim to foster discussion and debate, ultimately helping to advance the global movement of wellbeing.

Although consumer demand for wellbeing is at an all-time high, limited preconceptions of wellbeing can lead to it being seen as a niche luxury and the preserve of the privileged. However, the pandemic has shown that health and wellbeing aren't optional, they are the basis of a fulfilling life and fundamentally linked to the health of the planet. A successful future for people and planet would see wellbeing incorporated in every aspect of our lives, not just as individuals but in our connection to nature and each other. As we help to drive this global movement, we will increasingly see governments, society and companies buying in to our vision of 'wellbeing for all'.

Sauna culture is central to the DNA of the Therme experience and we already have an extraordinary level of expertise in this area. In commissioning this research, we wish to take our knowledge even further, exploring all of the world's bathing traditions, not only to inform our future developments, but to share our findings and help drive a new global culture of wellbeing, with the benefits of thermal bathing at its core.

The Covid-19 pandemic has given increased attention and urgency to preventative healthcare and wellbeing, particularly in the ever more populated urban environment. We believe there is a positive way forward, addressing some of the most pressing health challenges of our age and helping humans to thrive in harmony with nature. As we emerge from the pandemic, there will be a greater focus on helping individuals, communities and populations to have an increased level of all-round health, and resilience to future health challenges. We believe sauna and thermal bathing can contribute to that goal.

Through our current wellbeing resorts in Germany I have seen first-hand the profound wellbeing benefits of sauna therapy to our guests. In taking the concept to Bucharest, we have seen how quickly thermal bathing has been accepted and how it taps into the universal need for experiences based in water, heat and nature. Through this research we will help to bring meaningful sauna experiences to all of our guests worldwide.

At the centre of a former industrial port in Gothenburg, a strange corrugated-metal structure stands among the angular forms of cranes dotting the water's edge. The unknown structure is a free public sauna, Bathing Culture, designed by architects raumlabor. It is intended as a catalyst to spark community-led transformation of the area from disused port to a vibrant new residential and recreational district. Raumlabor's masterplan for Frihamnen, Gothenburg, is just one of a number of recent waterside regeneration projects that use a sauna as a focal point and community hub. Raumlabor understand that sauna is about more than simply sweating:

'Public baths were once an intense place for social gatherings in our cities. ... This has been lost in our cities and substituted with the more bleak and leisure-based public swimming pools and spas. We see the baths as a social space to meet people, spend time together and discuss life. The sensorial qualities of the baths provide us with a place where there is no competition, consumption or spectacle, but where the focus is purely on sharing spaces and thoughts, and enjoying and benefiting from the water.' raumlabor, 2015

The free public sauna by raumlabor in Gothenburg, Sweden, 2016. Image © raumlabor

This book began life as a research paper commissioned by Therme Group to promote a deeper contemporary understanding of sauna culture and wellbeing. Water, bathing culture and the sauna in particular are central to Therme and their vision of wellbeing for all, along with pioneering initiatives like Therme Forum – a cultural platform for debating art, nature and technology – and their role in supporting health for people and the planet.

Drawing on several decades of personal fascination with and research into global bathing cultures, our aim is to illuminate one of the most venerated communal bathing traditions and analyse why and how it is gaining new credence and relevance in our stressed and hyper-connected world. To explore how it is being reinvented as a therapeutic tool to support systemic wellbeing, as well as a powerful catalyst to building community and fostering connection with water and the natural world. Although sauna might seem a niche practice, it touches on myriad current topics such as physical and psychological wellbeing, identity, sexuality, ecology, nature, water resources and many more.

In the first section we go back to the roots of the sauna and take a deep dive into ancient customs to rediscover what authenticity means at a time when most saunas are pallid imitations of the real thing. Here we look to Finland and the Nordic region, which is still considered the heartland of sauna culture and where there is a deep-rooted desire to protect the sanctity of traditions and respect for the spiritual dimension of sauna. We also explore how renewed interest in ancient rituals and vernacular traditions is nourishing a new sauna consciousness. In particular the renaissance of the public sauna as an urban destination, a social and cultural space with a different tempo from the clothed world.

Concurrently, renewed interest in bathing culture has brought a spirit of invention and experimentation to sauna, especially in Asia. In chapter 5 we explore these new hybrids and see how designers are mixing steam with digital technologies to shape immersive experiences.

In chapter 8 we illuminate the potential for water therapies and sauna ritual to become an important part of a growing wellbeing culture. In the past, discussions about the health benefits of the sauna have tended to focus on hygiene, benefits to the immune system and cardiac health. But are there other aspects that resonate in today's liminal world? A return to the earthy and elemental, an intensely physical experience in contrast to our slippery digital environments? Fulfilling a longing for slowness? Countering anxieties with heat and steam? Can we analyse sauna experience and environments through this lens to deepen our understanding of the bond between design and wellbeing, and how this can be supported and enhanced?

During 2020 and the ongoing Covid-19 pandemic, saunas and other leisure facilities were closed for fear of infection. After the initial panic, many reopened with an understanding of how to prevent transmission, and the risk of contamination when social distancing is managed effectively is low. Recent research by leading sauna academics Jari Laukkanen and Setor Kunutsor suggests that regular Finnish sauna practice may help prevent Covid-19 infection. At the same time, there is growing interest and research into hygiene and a proactive approach to prevention of infection through design and materials. However, the pandemic has also increased awareness of our fundamental need for physical and mental wellbeing. During successive lockdowns many of us have felt keenly the loss of personal rituals such as sauna and their positive effects on our lives. Can this heightened understanding of our need for such rituals shine a light on the potential of sauna to play a greater role both in healing and preventative healthcare?

Like food, bathing culture is constantly evolving and finding a balance between tradition and experimentation, the local and the cosmopolitan. New takes on ancient bathing rituals are like adding new ingredients to spice up traditional dishes. When guided by an inspired chef or sauna pioneer, these fusions offer the thrill of new tastes without losing sight of the original. *Social Sauna* is envisaged as the first in a series of papers exploring global bathing cultures and how these living traditions can support wellbeing and community and help reframe our connection to the natural world at a time when it hangs in the balance.

Jane Withers

1. DEFINING THE ESSENCE OF SAUNA

Traditional Estonian smoke sauna. Estonia, Finland and Russia are the only countries with a continuous sauna culture. Image © Tönu Runnel

The sauna is one of the oldest and most enduring bathing cultures and one that is still defined by deep-rooted ideas of authenticity. But what does this mean for an ancient bathing tradition in today's world? Some of the most exhilarating recent expressions of sauna depart radically from traditional design vernacular, and yet capture sauna's 'essence' in a way that seems more resonant than others that are of traditional appearance and yet offer a hackneyed version of the sauna experience. Clearly notions of authenticity in bathing culture, as with food or craft, are subject to cultural context and are continuously evolving. We need to ask what is essential about sauna – its qualities and values – and how we can redefine a spirit that resonates for a 21st-century audience and social, cultural and environmental context. Here we set out some essential elements of sauna.

Primordial

→ The sauna resonates with the spirits of the ancients – pagan, earthy, tribal and animistic – connected to the forest, trees and wood as the living body of trees. It is a space that can take modern man back a thousand years to realise that much of what matters is still the same.

→ Having evolved as an arboreal species, humans have a profound subconscious affinity with the forest and the positive emotions that this connection sustains.

→ Recent scientific research and engagement with trees in the cultural sphere point towards a broader reappraisal of the value of forests.

Simplicity

→ In architectural terms, the sauna originates in simple structures – pits, dugouts, huts and rustic homesteads – utilitarian and yet infused with feeling and craftsmanship.

→ The savusauna, the most traditional smoke sauna, is little more than a pile of rocks in a log cabin, and the fire and water that bring it to life.

→ Vernacular sauna design is shaped by constraints: built from trees felled on the site, and wood kept as close to its natural state as possible.

→ The simple interior conjures an impression of life stripped down – like its users – to the bare necessities. It is a nucleus of survival, comfort and beauty.

→ With this lack of artifice comes a lack of distractions – visually and in textures and touch – a reset for the senses.

Architecture of the Senses

→ The way a sauna feels, sounds and smells overtakes the way things look; this haptic charge helps us to fully engage in the present and a phenomenological experience of space.

→ Sauna has a physical intensity: it is about extremes of fire and ice, it messes with our senses and perception. We lose ourselves in the moment, even experience disorientation.

→ Sauna is not really about the building, but about the building in use: the simple material triad of wood, steam and flesh.

→ Grounding and earthy, physically and mentally, through its elemental materials – wood, water and stone – the sauna takes us back into the realm of haptic experience and back into the body.

Nature

→ A profound connection to nature and coexistence with natural forces is embedded in the soul of sauna. The rural cabin deep within a forest or beside water is still a universal ideal.

→ The sauna is a place for experiencing nature – forest views, scents and sounds – and one's own nature; a connection that is all the more pronounced at a time when the conservation of the environment is at a tipping point.

→ The sauna offers an escape from the confines of (urban) life for fresh air and cold swims.

→ Sauna emphasises the authority of nature and its rhythms – the connection to night and day and the seasons.

Human

→ The sauna resonates because of its human scale and sense of being crafted by hand.
→ It is a catalyst for coming together, for people in the raw: a spreader of warmth and humanity.

Löyly

→ This is the sacred steam of the sauna; transformative and otherworldly.
→ An enveloping warmth that melts anxieties, tension and animosity.
→ A medium for myth as well as cleansing.

Fellowship

→ The sauna offers a protected and warm gathering place.
→ Whether it's for 2 people or 100, the bath is about balancing social behaviour, the individual and the communal.
→ The revival of the public sauna has emerged as a powerful social tool, building a sense of community.

Slow

→ Sauna slows down time and takes you into another dimension.
→ It is a place to escape the grip of the second hand and lose oneself in the present.

Detail of the stove, Mildred's Lane Sauna, Bauhaus Sauna Society, Pennsylvania, USA, 2012. Image © Felix Sattler

2. MYSTERIES OF STEAM

The Women's Bath, Follower of Albrecht Dürer, c. 1505/1510

Sauna is deeply ingrained in the culture of northern Europe, a ritual that has been handed down from one generation to the next countless times. Here we look briefly at sauna's roots and history in Europe, traditional sauna etiquette, and the mythology and spirituality associated with this ancient custom as a way of understanding what is still meaningful today.

Birth of Sauna

The origins of sauna are obscured by the mists of time as well as the mysticism engulfing what, for the Finns at least, is considered an almost religious rite. The Finns began their migration thousands of years ago from Central Asia across south-western Russia, central Europe and the Baltic states, to settle in what is now Finland. Although little is known about these nomadic people, it is likely they had some form of sweat bath, as did many others around the world. After all, capturing the heat of hot rocks is an efficient way to keep warm. Early baths are likely to have been portable – similar to the portable sweat lodge carried by some indigenous American peoples and still seen in Central Asia. By the Middle Ages, sweat baths were common across Europe, and Dürer's sketches reveal bathhouses in Nuremberg that are not dissimilar to saunas of a century ago. When the Reformation forced the closure of bathhouses across Europe, only the Finns, Russians and Estonians kept up the tradition, and they are still the keepers of this flame.

'Bain Finlandais', illustration of Finnish sauna, Giuseppe Acerbi, 1802

The Finnish Sauna

The Finns in particular have imbued sauna with an almost spiritual significance. In her essay *The Sauna*, June Pelo references a Swedish economist writing in 1776 'These stubborn people even connect the sauna with their theology and think the sauna building is some kind of shrine.' In the 19th century, as the national romantic movement shaped a distinctive Finnish cultural identity after centuries of Russian and Swedish rule, the sauna was enshrined in this rural idyll. In the Finnish epic folk tales of the Kalevala, gods take saunas and breathe löyly or steam. The Finns' reverence for this simple hut makes sense in the context of an inhospitable landscape pocked with frozen lakes and embalmed in gloom for much of the winter, when temperatures can drop as low as -50°C. In the documentary *Steam of Life* (2010), a portrait of Finnish male sauna culture, we see how the sauna is still a part of rural life inspiring comradeship and warming people in remote regions of a country that stretches far into the Arctic Circle. Sauna also fits the idea of sisu; considered by Finns to be their national characteristic, sisu has been described as a combination of determination, bravery and resilience, similar to the idea of 'having guts'.

The Nordic association of the sauna with family and kinship has also protected it from becoming sexualised in the way that happened to the bathhouses of medieval Europe, 18th century spa towns in England or bathhouses in America in the mid-twentieth century and Aids era and led to their censure and closure.

Despite a deep attachment to vernacular traditions, the sauna has evolved with Finland's changing social and cultural context. Although the rustic hut on a granite rock surrounded by water and an enchanted forest remains an ideal, as we see in chapter 3, the sauna has also become a site for experimentation and other powerful models are emerging.

The rise of the urban public sauna began in the 19th century with the population shift to the city. A century ago in Helsinki there was a public sauna on every block; these were the city's social clubs. Most closed during a period of rapid post-war redevelopment as the invention of the electric sauna heater made it possible to shoe-horn wooden boxes into apartment blocks. This decline is now being reversed as the public sauna is reinvented as an urban destination (see chapter 4). The sauna has long attracted experimentation as a micro-architecture capable of embodying a profoundly humanistic ethos, as Alvar Aalto demonstrated, but these new urban bathhouses are giving the sauna renewed prominence as social and architectural landmarks.

Helsinki sauna, early 20th century.

The Ten Commandments of the Bather

In 1944, the Finnish Union of Commercial Saunas issued 'The Ten Commandments of the Bather' to be displayed in all public saunas as a guide to instruct Finns and refugees newly arriving in cities in the post-war period. These instructions, excerpts of which are shown below, are still relevant today in revealing the Finns' relationship to sauna, and as a guide to sauna behaviour.

→ Behave well in the sauna at all times, as it is a 'sacred' place according to the ways of our ancestors.
→ Do not come to the sauna intoxicated, or bring intoxicating substances.
→ Take enough steam, but do not spoil the sauna of others by excessive 'athletic' steam pouring. In the sauna, use as little water as possible – a 'drier' steam is more pleasurable for you and your co-bathers. Do not soften your whisk on the stove, as it may produce undesirable odours and spoil your whisk's aroma.
→ Do not use any soap in the sauna, as its slipperiness has caused many unfortunate accidents. Do not take bottles or other glass objects into the washing hall or sauna, as they will cause injuries if they shatter.
→ Wash yourself thoroughly, but do not use water wastefully. Fill your bucket first with cold water before dispensing a suitable amount of hot water. After washing, take a shower, but do not stay there long, as there are others waiting for their turn. Do not splash or sprinkle your washing water onto others.

Quoted by Tuomas Toivonen in 'The Ten Commandments of the Public Bath', *Well, Well, Well, Harvard Design Magazine*, no. 40, 2015

Mythology and Ritual

'If a sick person is not cured by tar, spirits or sauna, then they will die.'

Finnish proverb

The rustic poetry of the sauna emanates from the mysteries of steam, as well as the rich seams of sauna folklore and Northern mythologies. The sauna features in the Finnish folk epic the Kalevala and is one of the ordeals of the Nine Worlds of Norse mythology that are connected by Yggdrasil, the cosmic tree that stretches from the celestial, deep into the earth. Known as the poor man's apothecary, the sauna is the site of medicine, healing, transformation and purification rituals, and a place for ancestor worship. With the ritual of pouring hot water onto the fiery stones to produce löyly, the sauna is often likened to a shrine, with the stove as its altar. The direct translation of löyly is steam, but the word also carries deeper meanings of living breath and evokes ancestors. The quality of a sauna is judged by its löyly – the balance of humidity, its taste, and the way it embraces the bather and feels on the skin. Sauna is still practised as an esoteric ritual by shamans to summon spirits, honouring the powers of the elements – fire, water and stone (earth) – and bringing them together to create a löyly imbued with magic, thought to be the very breath of the earth and the ancestors. In folklore, bathers must respect sauna and banya (Russian bathhouse) spirits or they will be plagued by their mischievous antics.

Sauna Huginn & Muninn by AtelierFORTE, Piacenza, Italy, 2012, takes inspiration from Odin's ravens in Norse mythology. Image © AtelierFORTE

Spirit of Sauna

In the Northern Shamanic tradition, the sauna is a sacred purification ritual for individuals or community gatherings, the beginning of which is described below. As the löyly builds, the shaman describes the feeling as more than physical, a full-body experience that makes the spine tingle. It is this sensation that sauna-bathers still seek today.

> 'Start by placing the stones on the oven, and feel the shape of each one. Appreciate their stone-ness, and their earthiness, and ask the spirit of the Earth beneath your feet to bless them. Then touch the water in its bucket ... and ask the spirits of all the cold northern rivers and lakes to bless it. Then light the fire, preferably with flint and steel or an even older method. As you do this, ask the fire to bless and cleanse you. Sing to it if you can because it likes song ... Wait patiently while the fire warms the room and stones. Whisper just loud enough for you to hear: "From Fire and Stone ... all creation".'
>
> 'Northern Traditions Sauna' from Raven Kaldera, *Wightridden: Paths of Northern Tradition Shamanism*

These rituals have been re-interpreted by contemporary practitioners, including the Bauhaus Sauna Society. Alexander Markus Lembke, founding member of the society, says 'I aim to encapsulate and express the lively tradition, radical change and current reality of sauna bathing. Resisting the urbanisation and technological penetration of Northern European society, this tradition has been lovingly maintained as an island of original human interaction with nature and temperature.'

Bauhaus Sauna Society observe and record these rituals, as well as developing their own with a deep respect for the vernacular spirit.

Contemporary sauna rituals created during the 'Expedition Exhibition – defining the 21st century explorer' project, Bauhaus Sauna Society, Kemijärvi, Finland, 2011. Image © Alexander Lembke

Lusthoone Sauna by Peeter Pere Arhitektid, Varbola Estonia, 2019. A new zig-zag roof protects the traditional sauna and creates sheltered exterior space. Image © Tõnu Runnel

3. LEARNING FROM THE VERNACULAR

Part of the sauna's resonance today is its sense of connection to a living vernacular and primordial ritual. In our world of steel, concrete, glass and cyber waves, the appeal of the primitive wooden cabin – its simplicity of design and raw physicality of experience – touches on myriad current ideas about ecology, nature, nostalgia, holistic wellbeing and much more. Here we explore vernacular sauna design and notions of authenticity, analysing why and how this is inspirational today. Traditional sauna design is deeply rooted in the natural world through the trees used to construct the building and fuel the stove, through the location deep in nature, and through time-honoured ritual that forges a bond with ancient times. It is this link to our predecessors that resonates today, a feeling that deep down we are not so different from our forebears and can, for a moment at least, share their knowledge of the primeval and the spirits of nature.

As we seek to understand authenticity in sauna design, the haptic and atmospheric qualities of the vernacular sauna are all the more relevant. Traditional saunas are constructed by following ancestral knowledge that brings together the essential elements of sauna in harmony – heat, light, smell, material, orientation, construction detail and the all-important löyly – to create a rich sauna-bathing experience.

This section analyses these roots and suggests ways in which they can be reinterpreted. Saunas in this section are organised according to four attributes: smoke, which imbues the earliest wood-fired saunas built before the invention of the chimney and is still revered today; earth, as the building material of the most primitive saunas and also the grounding experience of the sauna; communality, symbolising human connection through a shared bathing ritual; and retreat, the sauna as a place of stillness, contemplation and transformation.

Alvar Aalto at his smoke sauna at Muuratsalo, Finland, 1952–53. Muuratsalo was Aalto's experimental summer house where he tested different materials, construction techniques, forms and proportions. Image © Alvar Aalto Foundation

Smoke

'Whether I hung my clothes on a tree or on a coat hanger, I was never disappointed by a savusauna. Their sooted walls emanate the savory smells of wood, earth and camaraderie. Steam reaches out from the rocks like friendly hands, dispensing their heat. The bather warms evenly, everywhere at once. With my senses warm and smiling, my mind easily drifted into reverie.'

Mikkel Aaland, *Sweat*, 1978

The savusauna or smoke sauna is still considered the quintessential sauna experience by many, and the cabin darkened by decades of soot and permeated by the warm smell of wood smoke remains an ideal.

Conceived before the invention of the chimney, when the fire is lit, smoke remains in the room during the heating process, giving this type of sauna its name. Once the stove is fiery hot, the embers are extinguished and the smoke is released, soot washed from the benches and the sauna can begin. The savusauna ritual is an antidote to today's busy world: it demands patience and attention to heat the stones over several hours, during which the fire must be skilfully and regularly fuelled and checked to ensure a steady, safe burn.

Historically, the sauna was the first building to be built in a new settlement and had multiple uses as an essential place of warmth and cleansing as well as being a place to malt barley, cure meat, smoke fish and clean flax. The antibacterial properties of the carbon particles in soot made the sauna the cleanest place in the home, a place for giving birth and for medical treatment and rituals. Renewed understanding of hygiene is more relevant than ever as we counter the effects and fear of infection during the Covid-19 pandemic.

To ensure the bather is enveloped from head to toe in löyly, specific dimensions were developed and in traditional saunas the door height is as low as 80 cm, causing bathers to bow humbly as they enter the sauna. The top of the stove is at least 10 cm above the top of the door, and 10 cm below the foot platform. When the door is opened, the steam cannot escape, creating a constant pocket of pleasant, soft löyly.

Kiuas

In its most primitive form, the kiuas or stove is simply a carefully balanced pile of volcanic stones with a hollow under the centre for the fire. Igneous rocks and granite are heat-resistant and most suitable for sauna use, and were usually gathered from the closest local source. Today, cement adds stability to the structure but the principle remains the same. The kiuas will stay hot for several days, starting at an almost unbearable heat on the first day and gradually cooling to a temperature similar to that of a hammam by the third. Water must be poured very gently onto the stones in the same spot to create a soft steam – if care is not taken, the steam can scorch like a whip. A traditional smoke sauna is heated from 70–85°C at 12–30% humidity – without the temperature control of an electric heater, there is great variation between individual saunas. An opportunity for bathers to make löyly themselves is an essential component of the sauna experience.

Modern sauna stoves can be easily and accurately heated to as much as 110°C and sauna-bathers can only withstand this extreme heat if the humidity is very low, at around 4%. However, most saunas aren't as hot as this and a common temperature is around 90°C. Sauna expert Lassi A. Liikkanen believes that saunas have become hotter and dryer as technology has advanced. In the context of Covid-19, research published in the Lancet has demonstrated that high sauna temperatures of more than 70°C are effective at killing virus particles in 3-5 minutes, and in 1 minute at 80°C. When social distancing is managed carefully and those with symptoms do not attend sauna sessions, sauna is therefore a comparatively safe activity.

Finnish wartime dugout sauna, 1942

Subterranean

Storfinnhova Gård sauna, Kimito Island, Finland. Image © Storfinnhova Gård

The first saunas were underground or dugout saunas, in common use until the Iron Age, when log construction became more sophisticated. Usually dug into a hillside, with a log roof covered by turf and a wooden façade, the earthen walls provided insulation. The building contained only a pile of heated stones – to serve as a primitive stove – and a log bench, and sometimes doubled as a simple dwelling. Today, only a few traditional underground saunas remain and those that are still in use are valued as an exceptional experience.

Described as one of the most beautiful smoke saunas in Finland, Storfinnhova Gård is dug into the hillside, and constructed with massive granite blocks and logs. It is situated in the forest next to a stream, which partly flows through the sauna forming two pools. Bathers can take a cooling dip in the lower pool, and the constant sound of water is calming. The feeling of descending into the earth and being enveloped in its immutable silence is physically and mentally grounding.

Retreat

Collecting water for the sauna, Midsummer's Eve, Finland, 1963. Image © Finnish Heritage Agency

Part of the appeal of the vernacular sauna is the sense of refuge and sanctuary either through a secluded location, or simply by retreating within. The remote lakeside or forest sauna immersed in nature generates a ritualistic sense of calm and a connection to the natural world – a desire for which has grown as humans have become distanced from nature. The typical sauna retreat is imagined as a rural summer house in which to reset urban lives. Bathers are free to follow their personal sauna journey from heat to cool as many times as they want, in touch with how their body feels, and ignoring the clock.

Communality

At its heart, the sauna is a communal experience where people come together to share the social ritual. This can be a rural gathering in a family savusauna, a neighbourhood village sauna, or the larger public saunas that became prevalent in Nordic towns and cities after wood-fired stoves with chimneys made town-centre saunas safer in the 18th century. Usually, saunas were a weekly meeting point for the community to sit together in silence and wash away the week's cares, or to discuss politics and gossip. Today, the appeal of this social dimension is a catalyst for the revival of the public sauna.

Public saunas were common in Finnish towns until the 1950s, when the rise of the electric stove enabled private saunas to proliferate in family homes and apartment blocks. A huge decline from over 100 public saunas in Helsinki to only 3 at the turn of the last century has been partially reversed with the recent sauna revival among a younger generation. There are around 10 public saunas in the city today, many still in residential communities such as Kotiharju public sauna, which has been operating since the 1930s. Towel-wrapped bathers spill out onto the street to cool off, showing a relaxed approach to the body. However, a new type of landmark sauna has also emerged, which we examine in more detail in chapter 4.

Kotiharju public sauna,
Helsinki, Finland.
Image © Helsinki Marketing/
Jussi Hellsten

The Order of the Bath

Today as sauna has become a global activity, those who haven't grown up with sauna customs aren't familiar with the entire process. Here we set out a typical savusauna practice which can be adapted and followed at any sauna. The most important elements are the sequence of the hot sauna followed by a swift cool down to be repeated a couple of times, and also taking enough time to enjoy the entire ritual.

1. Take time to prepare the sauna. Heat the stove and tend the fire for several hours. Once hot, release the smoke, and wash the soot from the benches.

2. Wash or shower before sauna.

3. On entering the sauna, ask if you can make some steam and gently ladle water using a 'kippo' onto the hot stones.

4. Stay in the sauna until you can bear the heat no longer (this varies, 10–15 minutes or longer).

5. Use a vihta, a bundle of leafy birch twigs soaked in warm water, to 'whisk' or gently beat the skin, increasing blood circulation and perspiration and producing a forest aroma.

6. Use the vihta in the second round once the skin has softened.

7. Follow the intense heat of the sauna by a cold dip – in the sea, lake, plunge pool, shower or rolling in the snow.

8. Rest and cool down outdoors before the next session.

9. Repeat several times as desired.

10. Take a final rinse or shower.

11. Relax in a warm place, preferably around a fire.

12. Have a cool drink and something to eat, continuing discussions begun in the sauna.

A vihta, or sauna whisk, from the series Spirit of Sauna by Esa Ylijääskö, 2017. Image © Esa Ylijääskö

FLYT Sauna, Rintala Eggertsson, Moss, Norway, 2020. Image © Nicholas Ryan Coates

4. CONTEMPORARY SAUNA

Since the beginning of the 21st century, sauna culture has evolved radically as designers experiment with form and experience, instigating what has been described as a sauna renaissance. As we will see here, at one end of the spectrum architects are thoughtfully revisiting vernacular traditions and using this micro-architecture as a ground for exploring a profoundly humanistic architecture. At the other end is the revival and transformation of the public sauna into a temple to a new bathing culture. Others take a grassroots approach and community focus, or appropriate a DIY/hacker ethos in the pursuit of steam, resulting in unexpected and delightful experiences. Here we also take a brief look at global sauna interpretations, and how other cultures have developed their own sweat-bathing customs.

As well as documenting these new approaches, we question why the sauna as social experience should be so resonant today, whether through the allure of a communal interaction with a different tempo to the clothed world, an intensely physical experience, or a place to disconnect from the digital and re-immerse in the real.

Lonna sauna by OOPEAA, Helsinki, Finland, 2016. Image © Julia Kivela

Reinterpreting the Vernacular

Since Alvar Aalto and the birth of the modern sauna, architects and designers have enjoyed exploring how to recreate the typology in a contemporary way and yet remain faithful to the vernacular in spirit and function. The saunas discussed here foreground materiality, making and craft, and a rejuvenating connection to nature. With a respect for materials and resources, either through adaptive reuse of a building or in the ecological approach to fuelling the sauna, every aspect of these saunas has been carefully considered, contributing to a holistic and mindful sauna journey and a deep sense of connection to people and the environment.

Villa Mairea

Alvar Aalto

Noormarkku
Finland, 1937–39

Above: The turf-roofed sauna building contrasts with the organic form of the pool at Villa Mairea. Right: Japanese and African influences can be seen in the details of the sauna building. Images © Alvar Aalto Foundation

For Alvar Aalto, as for many Finns, the sauna was more than simply a bath, it was a ritual space where the physical and spiritual come together. This small but important category occupies a significant place in Aalto's work and he designed around 30 saunas during his lifetime for public, private and institutional use. In 1925, he wrote solemnly about the search for a new cultural sauna in Finland, describing it as if it were a temple; 'So let's build a sauna there! Not a standard Finnish sauna, like all our saunas, but a cultural sauna, a national monument, the first of its kind in Finland's awakening civilisation.' The sauna at Villa Mairea is perhaps Aalto's best known. The pavilion by the pool is connected to the main house by a loggia with a flat turf roof. A collage of various elements and influences, the sauna is a symbolically charged feature in a building that is representative of Aalto's softer interpretation of Modernism, which brought together references as varied as Modernist architecture and painting, Finnish vernacular buildings, as well as Japanese and African influences.

Tonttu Sauna   OOPEAA   Finland, 2010

The building is an adaptive reuse of a 19th-century granary, which was derelict for 50 years before being renovated and transformed into a new sauna. Rotten timbers were replaced and new elements of honey-coloured spruce were added which will eventually develop a patina and merge with the old. The building's functions are distributed vertically within the space according to temperature requirements. Sauna bathing takes place on the hot mezzanine platform which echoes traditional sauna design and where the entire body of the bather can be enveloped in löyly. Washing and resting take place at lower, cooler levels. There are two ways to cool down: by relaxing on the sheltered lower terrace, or by heading up to the wooden plunge pool.

Savusauna Joensuu   Tuomo Siitonen   Asikkala, Finland, 2016

At only 27 m² this savusauna is a tiny haven in a remote lakeside location without modern distractions. Built by master craftspeople working closely with the architect, the sauna is beautifully detailed to create a minimal exterior, articulated by horizontal 'salmon head' log joints. Rawness is expressed through the massive timber construction – the logs are the width of the tree. Situated high above a lake, with a view through the trees and across the water, the setting cossets the bather in nature, while the soft steam of the smoke sauna and the descent from the sauna to the cooling lake below are a salve for the body and the mind.

Images © Rauno Träskelin

Bathhouse Explorers

'More than creating a space for physical bathing, the architecture of the bath requires – and creates – a space of anti-conflict, anti-competition, and anti-hierarchy. The space of communal bathing is enclosed, civil, and polite; every bather autonomously performs his or her own version of an agreed set of practices, without interfering with others.'

Tuomas Toivonen, *Well, Well, Well, Harvard Design Magazine*, no. 40, 2015

Since the early 20th century, sauna has been understood by many as more than simply a place to bathe; it is a place of reverie and a reset for the soul. But somewhere along the way, that understanding was obscured, and as we have discussed, saunas became for the most part insipid imitations of the real thing. Since the mid-1970s, a few key figures pioneered a revival in bathing culture, and they are still influential today in driving the new sauna movement.

In 1978, Mikkel Aaland, a Norwegian-American photographer and author, wrote the seminal book, *Sweat,* which has become a bible for bathing enthusiasts and helped nurture a renewed appreciation for the practice. Aaland is revisiting the subject of his original book in a new documentary series *Perfect Sweat* which explores global sauna cultures including Finnish, Russian banya, Turkish hammam and Japanese mushi-buro. Aaland, with the help of local guides and presenters, persuades viewers that sauna is fundamental to wellbeing.

Another extraordinarily influential figure is Leonard Koren, founder of *Wet: The Magazine of Gourmet Bathing,* published from 1976–1981, which now has cult status. For Koren, the bath is 'a place that awakens me to my intrinsic earthly, sensual and paganly reverential nature. A quiet place to enjoy one of life's finest desserts amidst elemental surroundings.' In his book *Undesigning the Bath,* 1996, Koren suggested that only a handful of designer baths were not 'oppressively sterile, boring, or mannerist caricatures of some historical model.'

The work of bathing thinkers and experimenters like Aaland and Koren has been inspirational to a new generation of sauna enthusiasts who are reinventing sauna culture and design for the 21st century. They harness the power of sauna as a focal point for new public bathing experiences that embrace the Roman ideal of the bathhouse as a place to balance body and mind, as well as creating the elemental bathing environments that Koren sought.

When imagining a new public sauna in Helsinki, architects Tuomas Toivonen and Nene Tsuboi of NOW Office were inspired by the sauna writings of Alvar Aalto, as well as the Roman bathhouse, which incorporated learning, exercise and bathing. Attached to their studio, Toivonen and Tsuboi describe Kulttuurisauna, completed in Helsinki, 2012, as 'a special social and architectural space, a combination of baths with a social space enabling cultural activity, production and exchange'.

Norwegian-based Finnish architect Sami Rintala has forged a path as a sauna specialist, creating many projects where the sauna is a focal point for communal space fused with architectural experimentation. His sauna for SALT Arts Festival, designed with partner Dagur Eggertsson, is now permanently installed in Oslo and and is proving a catalyst to a resurgence in bathing culture in Norway. The site is home to saunas with different scales and atmospheres, and Rintala describes the experience as a social sauna subculture. 'SALT has concerts and lectures. It can be a "proper" hot sauna experience or a cultural happening. It becomes a carnivalistic way of using a sauna, or the traditional way of being in your own thoughts.'

Rintala describes his self-built mountain sauna as the most profound experience and does not allow it to be published in order to protect it from sauna tourists. He is working on saunas across Norway including the ARK floating sauna system, and Forest Spa with three saunas immersed in the forest – a savusauna, a sauna on pillars in the tree canopy, and another with an onsen bath. Each project is a step closer to the ideal of bathing directly in nature.

It is these combined bathing and cultural spaces which take a holisitic view of wellbeing that Rintala considers the future of bathing and part of a wider Scandinavian and global sauna boom.

Solar Egg sauna by artists Bigert & Bergström was commissioned as a sculptural community focal point. Image © Bigert & Bergström

The New Sauna Mythology

In the last decade there has been a resurgence in communal sauna culture with the construction of new public saunas in Helsinki, and around the world. The most prominent of these are spectacular environments that reference and transform sauna traditions. The saunas in this section draw us towards their seductive architecture and intriguing spaces. They offer immersive experiences and stimulation for all the senses, social spaces that reset the connection between body and mind.

Some saunas are highly sophisticated in their execution, from the choice of materials to the thoughtful transition between spaces so that the visitor journey is seamless and comforting, or alternatively exhilarating and uplifting. Some are conceived as urban destinations with cafes and bars as well as sauna and wellness facilities, so the sauna is reintegrated as a steamy dimension to the fabric of urban life. The commercial facilities support the running of the sauna and also appeal to a new generation of sauna-goers who consider the sauna a social destination.

Outside the urban context, we have identified an emerging sauna typology that enables an encounter with the wild, and yet offers protection from the extremes of nature – a tempered wild. Designers are also taking inspiration from traditional ecological knowledge to create saunas and bathing structures that demonstrate a growing empathy with the environment.

Löyly Design Sauna by Avanto Architects, Helsinki, Finland, 2016. Image © Kuvio.com

Löyly Design Sauna

Avanto Architects

Helsinki, Finland, 2016

Löyly, Helsinki's most spectacular new public sauna, takes its name from the Finnish word both for the steam that radiates from sauna rocks when you sprinkle water over them, and also for the mystic spiritual dimensions of sauna. Designed to merge into the rocky waterfront, the sculptural slatted wooden canopy shelters the sauna building, creating a series of terraces over and around it. The cave-like interior houses a traditional smoke sauna and a wood-burning sauna, both bordering the Baltic where bathers cool off. The slow process of heating the wood-fired saunas is visible to visitors. Although its design is striking, Löyly retains the reductive, calm atmosphere found in traditional saunas as well as a strong connection to the sea. It has evolved from a sauna to a meeting place where one might go to eat in the restaurant, or meet for coffee, with or without going to the sauna.

Left: Löyly is surrounded by a slatted canopy that provides privacy and soft light to the saunas within. Image © Kuvio.com
Above right: Space for rest and relaxing after the sauna. Image © Mikko Ryhanen Joanna Laajisto Creative Studio
Below right: The savusauna's interior is blackened by smoke. Image © Kuvio.com

Bathing Culture   raumlabor   Gothenburg, Sweden, 2014

Above: Bathing Culture's larch shingle-lined sauna interior. Opposite: The corrugated-steel exterior. Images © raumlabor

'The sensorial qualities of the baths provide us with a place where there is no competition, consumption or spectacle, but where the focus is purely on sharing spaces and thoughts, and enjoying and benefiting from the water.'

raumlabor, 2015

Situated among the containers and cranes of Frihamnen, Gothenburg's former industrial port, Bathing Culture is intended as a catalyst for the area's regeneration and is free to use. It was conceived as a community project and the architects worked with local residents to build the sauna largely from reclaimed materials. The shower room is made of 1,200 recycled glass bottles and the sauna's powerful corrugated-steel exterior, which contrasts with the delicate larch shingle-lined sauna interior, references the area's industrial past. The sauna room has views across the water, bringing light and outside life inside.

Agora

Rintala Eggertsson
SALT Festival

Norway,
various locations,
2014–

Agora sauna is situated at the water's edge with a spectacular view of nature. Image © Martin Losvik

Four stoves are needed to heat the huge interior volume.
Image © Martin Losvik

The structure of Agora is inspired by traditional Norwegian fish-drying racks and was designed as a multi-purpose venue for festivals that can be assembled as one long structure or divided into smaller units. It can be adapted to different terrains, and is simple to assemble, pack up and transport to the next festival location. In its first iteration it was divided into three structures – a restaurant, a concert venue and a spacious sauna with capacity for 100 bathers. The bleacher-like seating offers a range of temperatures catering to different bathing preferences. The sauna has a lightweight cover to keep the steam in, echoing nomadic, temporary sauna and sweat lodge construction. It is now permanently installed on the Oslo waterfront, part of a SALT sauna and culture destination.

Solar Egg   Bigert & Bergström   Kiruna, Sweden, 2017

This golden egg-shaped sauna is made from irregular reflective metal panels, and stands like a futuristic beacon in the landscape, visible from afar. Inside, the harmonious circular space cocoons up to eight bathers, who have a view of the central human heart-shaped stove, and a link to the exterior world through the glass door. The circular form brings focus to the centre of the room and the bathing experience. The lightweight structure toured to different locations across Scandinavia and to Paris, before returning to Kiruna as a community asset.

Solar Egg's interior. Image © Bigert and Bergström

Solar Egg installed at Gällivare, Sweden, June 2018. Image © Bigert and Bergström

FLYT · Rintala Eggertsson Moss, Norway, 2020

FLYT sauna and diving platform connect the community to the sea. Image © Nicholas Ryan Coates

Rintala Eggertsson won a competition held by the municipality of Moss, Norway, to revitalise the town's former dock area for its 300-year anniversary. FLYT is a series of three sculptural pavilions with forms inspired by the surrounding industrial architecture including silos, cranes and gantries. The tallest of the pavilions is a diving platform with a light installation that represents the spectrum of colours of Norway's political parties as they come and go. The second pavilion is a free public sauna open year-round and the third is sited in a park set back from the waterfront. The sauna and diving platform are built on pre-existing piers and act as gateways to the sea, creating opportunities for the local community to bathe in and have a greater connection to the water. By contributing sculptural and functional elements to the public space, Rintala Eggertsson bring new energy to the area.

Steam of Life Pavilion

JKMM Architects with Sauna on Fire Collective

Burning Man Festival, USA, 2019

Conceived as a temporary installation for the desert festival, in this building bathers follow a circular journey from the changing area to the sauna and finally to the meditative central relaxation area. Made using two sizes of plywood panels and three timber-slat modules, the sauna can be flat-packed to fit into a 20-ft shipping container. Adapting to the desert climate, a shaded atrium takes the place of a lake or pile of snow to dip into, and the open structure becomes a lantern at night. Responding to the festival's theme of metamorphosis, the sauna's function of spiritual and physical cleansing and regeneration is embodied in its circular spaces where rituals evoking the cycles of life, death and the natural world can take place.

Image © Hannu Rytky

Grotto Sauna   Partisans   Lake Huron, Canada, 2014

This private sauna is constructed using sophisticated digital design techniques. In order to understand the complex age-old rock formations of the location and to build respectfully without damaging them, the team scanned the site with a laser to create a meticulous 3D computer model to inform the sauna's design. Digital design and construction methods enabled a low-impact construction and the creation of curvaceous organic forms. A simple black box exterior fits to the rock face, and belies its sculptural, grotto-like interior, made of locally sourced reclaimed cedar formed into curved panels, which imbue the atmosphere with their aromatic smell. A large rounded window punctuates the façade with a view towards the lake.

Grotto Sauna interior by Partisans. Image © Jonathan Friedman

Grotto Sauna fits snugly into the irregular surface of the rock it sits on. Image © Jonathan Friedman

The Tempered Wild

Sky Lagoon by Pursuit, Kársnes, Iceland, 2021. Image © Christopher Lund

A new typology of outdoor landscaped water retreat is emerging, that is designed to allow bathers to experience a seemingly untamed environment. Here leisurely sauna ritual is part of a larger water journey mediated through protective architecture that brings a degree of comfort and reassurance to the 'wild' experience. One example is Sky Lagoon, sited on the craggy coastline just outside Reykjavik. It offers restorative spa rituals rooted in Icelandic traditions and a geothermal lagoon at the ocean's edge where bathers can vicariously enjoy ocean views and the northern lights even as temperatures plunge. Another example of the tempered wild is True Blue a waterfront park and sea bath by White Arkitekter, where residents of Bergen will be able to commune with water throughout the year.

Inspired by TEK

Designers are waking up to the power of Traditional Ecological
Knowledge (TEK) and engaging with the 'Lo-TEK' design movement,
researched extensively by designer and academic Julia Watson.
Lo-TEK aims to 'rebuild an understanding of indigenous philosophy
and vernacular architecture that generates sustainable, climate-
resilient infrastructures'. A fertile ground for putting some of these
ideas into practice is in temporary experimental structures at
festivals. Examples of this approach include the Bathing Pavilions at
Wonderfruit Festival by Ab Rogers Design. The network of floating
pavilions was inspired by traditional Thai fishing villages. Each
bamboo shell is subtly different, creating dappled light of varying
softness according to its function. The pavilions were connected by a
series of pontoons supported by re-used polyethylene barrels.

Bathing Pavilions at Wonderfruit Festival by Ab Rogers Design, Thailand, 2019. Image © Wonderfruit

Panorama Wilderness Sauna by Bauhaus Sauna Society, Hamburg, Germany, 2017. Image © Alexander Lembke

Ad Hoc

The ad hoc or temporary sauna is an ancient and nomadic typology that continues today as designers enjoy experimenting with what can be created in a light-touch, inventive and playful spirit. These DIY structures tend to appear when people are at a temporary location, as in the military or at a festival, or stem from a simple desire to create one's own sauna. Often low-budget and using reclaimed materials, saunas can be made by hacking boats or trailers. Some of these saunas, such as Sompasauna in Helsinki, were built by anarchist communities without permission from either the landowner or the authorities. As off-grid structures, they are models for easy-to-make, low-impact construction, often using minimal resources. In their experimental approach, some of these projects capture an unexpected magic, as they float, fly or nestle into place.

The Finnish Rooftop Sauna

Aalto University Students and Jaakko Pernu

London, 2018

Images © India Roper-Evans

This popular pop-up winter sauna initiated by The Finnish Cultural Institute was built on the rooftop of the Southbank Centre, overlooking the Thames. While the sauna was housed in a translucent box, bathers cooling down on the terraces experienced the unusual feeling of being naked in the city centre. The views across London gave a fresh perspective on the city, lifting urban experience out of the ordinary. The bathing ritual was skilfully guided by a sauna expert to initiate those less familiar with the experience.

Sompasauna

Helsinki, Finland, 2011–present

Sompasauna is a free, volunteer-run and self-service sauna. If you arrive and the stove isn't lit, light it yourself. Made of found materials and rough around the edges, no one knows who first built it at the edge of land set for redevelopment. The first illegal iteration was destroyed by the authorities, but after a public outcry a series of replacement saunas have been tolerated due to the sanctity of the sauna in Finland, and have now secured local approval.

A sub-culture has developed around Sompasauna, and the community maintains the sauna and hosts a summer party. This DIY culture is part of a wider 'Kaupunkiaktiivisuus', or citizen activism movement, which also includes annual days where anyone can set up their own market stall or restaurant, and which particularly appeals to the millennial generation. Finland also celebrates National Sauna Day when anyone can open their sauna to visitors.

Image © Eetu Ahanen

DIY

Modern takes on ancient nomadic sweat baths are often seen in military saunas and in the backwoods. The Finnish military are renowned for constructing saunas wherever they are based and their dedication to sauna has been replicated by sauna lovers everywhere, who have transformed every imaginable space into saunas, from combine harvesters to telephone boxes.

As we have seen previously, designers and architects enjoy trialling these small structures, and the Czech office H3T Architekti have become known for the rich vein of sauna experimentation that runs through their practice. They have designed all kinds of temporary mobile, floating and flying saunas. Their playful approach brings a sense of joy and discovery, and a realisation that anything goes in sauna experience, so long as the löyly is good.

Converted combine harvester sauna, still from *Steam of Life*, 2010, directed by Joonas Berghäll and Mika Hotakainen, produced by Oktober. Image © Joonas Berghäll/OKTOBER

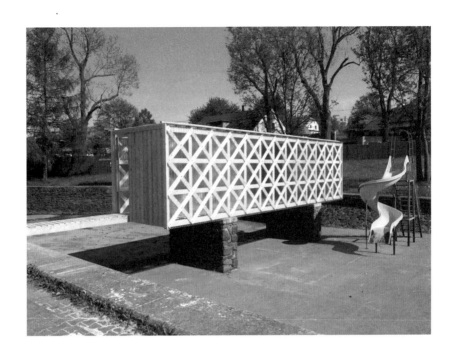

Experimental saunas by H3T
Architekti, clockwise from top:
Sauna Bridge, 2018; Cycloson
Kolonok, 2011; Flying Sauna,
2010; Cyklosauna Kolonok, 2011.
Images © H3T Architekti

On the Water

Saunas and water are natural companions, and designers have sought to enhance that relationship, along with tranquility and a sense of isolation, by creating experimental saunas on the water that can be accessed by boat, a swim or by walkway.

The floating VALA sauna is hidden in the wilderness of Soomaa National Park, Estonia, a riparian landscape that regularly floods. As the sauna travels along the streams, the relationship between water and the sauna ritual is accentuated by the surrounding landscape. The workshop project was designed to encourage student designers to consider and understand the many variables that contribute to a good sauna experience, including the challenges of dealing with fire and ventilation, with an achievable and enjoyable end result.

VALA sauna by Sami Rintala and Hannes Praks with Estonia Academy of Arts, Estonia, 2017. Image © Sami Rintala / Mari Hunt

Badeschiff, Wilk-Salinas Architekten, Berlin, Germany, 2005. Image © Torsten Seidel

In the city, barges have sometimes been transformed into saunas, as an inexpensive, sturdy and mobile foundation on which to build. Fitting into the urban waterscape, barges are an important part of the cityscape and its industrial history. A good example is the Badeschiff pool, built into the hull of an old barge in Berlin. It is designed to bring life to a neglected riverbank and allow people to enjoy swimming as close to the river as possible. Each winter, the Badeschiff pool and bar area is covered with an inflatable structure to allow swimming to continue, and a sauna is added to counter the winter climate. Similarly, in Prague, H3T Architekti annually transform the deck of a barge into a temporary sauna in the heart of the city.

Lázně na Lodi (Spa on the Boat) by H3T Architekti, Prague, Czech Republic, 2013–present. Image © H3T Architekti

Two women take a Hanjeungmak charcoal kiln bath in Hoengseong, South Korea. Image © Woohae Cho

Global Sweat Cultures

Forms of sweat bathing developed independently across the globe thousands of years ago. While these traditions died off in many parts of the world with the rise of plumbed water, several cultures have continued the idea of sweat bathing and sauna, and tailored these rituals for contemporary life.

In Korea, the jimjilbang, or bathhouse, hosts hot pools as well as kiln-like domed saunas of different temperatures, the interiors sometimes covered in healing materials such as salt or jade. Today, some Jimjilbang entrepreneurs are creating new approaches to bathing, while others are reawakening rural traditions as these practices are taken up by Korean communities around the world.

There has long been a cultural affinity between Finland and Japan in bathing as well as design. Japan has an ancient and revered onsen tradition that grew out of the country's thermal geology and wealth of hot springs. As we will see, the Japanese have also developed their own distinctive sweat rituals.

In the Americas, the Temezcal sweat culture emphasises spiritual renewal. Along with the sweat lodge ceremony of Indigenous peoples, this ancient custom of the Aztecs is being opened up to a broader audience today, as the benefits of these rituals become better understood.

South Korea

Korea's traditional form of sweat bathing, Hanjeungmak, takes place in kilns used for charcoal making. Twelve hours after the charcoal is taken out of the fiery clay-lined kiln, a wooden base is set inside and male and female bathers sit in the heat that reaches almost 200°C, hair protected by towels and wearing cotton clothing. Koreans' ancient belief in the healing properties of clay, in particular for women after giving birth, and in charcoal for purification have helped keep the popularity of kiln bathing alive. Pine needles or mugwort leaves may be spread on the floor of the kiln for their healing properties. Mugwort is recognised as a curative herb across Asia and Europe and is one of the nine sacred Nordic herbs. In Asia, it is used in acupuncture and valued for its powerful benefits for women's health. The kiln was also used as a place of meditation by Buddhist monks. Today, this modest sweat bath offers a way to reconnect with ancestral traditions.

Jimjilbang

The jimjilbang is a modern mash-up of the Japanese bathhouse, the Hanjeungmak or kiln sauna, and the western spa, in a new typology of large-scale leisure facility that was first launched in Seoul in 1992 and has quickly spread across South Korea. Jimjilbangs are usually found in malls, stations and leisure parks and operate 24/7. Bathers wear a cotton 'uniform' and wrap their towels to make yang mori 'lamb head' hats to protect their heads from the intense heat. Ajummas, or 'aunties', offer no-nonsense full-body scrubs. Today, the jimjilbang has been exported to Korean communities across the USA.

Aquafield   Roito and 16A   Hanam, South Korea, 2016

Aquafield is one the most inventive contemporary jimjilbangs, where visitors can sample pools and themed saunas. Situated in the Starfield Mall on the outskirts of Seoul, the rooftop pool overlooks the Han river. Saunas include a charcoal-lined Korean dry sauna and a salt-lined sauna. The walls of the Forest Room are clad in aromatic cypress wood accompanied by a large-scale projection of a forest. In the low-temperature Cloud Room, overleaf, bathers can play with the vapour streams cascading from the walls. The mirrored ceiling and glossy black walls play on ideas on infinity. This transfixing multi-sensory experience is part entertainment and part meditation.

This modern take on the ancient kiln sauna by Roito and 16A is lined with purifying charcoal. Aquafield, Hanam, South Korea, 2016. Image © Satoshi Awakawa and Yasushi Nagai

Cloud Room at Aquafield by Roito and 16A, Hanam, South Korea. Image © Satoshi Awakawa and Yasushi Nagai

The Americas

First peoples across the Americas developed their own sweat bathing rituals. There are similarities between the North American sweat lodge and the central American temazcal, but both are gaining a new relevance in supporting mental wellbeing today.

Temazcal

Dating from Aztec times, temazcal is introspective journey during which participants undergo a powerful spiritual renewal or rebirth. Guided by a shaman or temazcalera, the ceremony symbolises a passage between the heavens and the underworld, cleansing the mind, body and spirit, through which participants are brought to a heightened state of spiritual awareness.

Before the ceremony, an altar is made to acknowledge each element of earth, air, fire and water. Thick fragrant smoke of burning copal resin is wafted over each participant in a purification ritual. The low, dark space of the temazcal intensifies the atmosphere, which becomes increasingly hot and humid, up to 90°C as hot rocks are slowly added from the fire outside. The darkness allows the mind to roam as the senses of sound, touch and smell are stimulated by the shaman's chanting and the aromatic, healing herbs such as basil, mint, rosemary and sage which are infused in the water used to douse the hot stones.

Inipi

The Indigenous American sweat lodge has been used for meditative, transcendental and purification rituals since ancient times. Indigenous Nations have distinct rituals and one of the best-known is the Lakota people's sacred Inipi. The rite is led by elders who undergo years of training and are versed in the arts of native language, song and storytelling; they also ensure the safety of the participants. Sixteen saplings are bent to form a dome and covered with animal skins or blankets. Like temazcal, purification takes place before the ceremony, then scorching hot rocks are taken from the fire and put in the centre of the Inipi. The sacred herbs sage, sweetgrass and copal are burnt during the rite. As a sacred ceremony, the sweat lodge must be led only by Indigenous elders, but is occasionally opened to the public.

Japanese Sweat Bathing

The Japanese sauna developed quite separately from the Nordic sauna. Various Japanese saunas are referred to in documents from the 9th century onwards, but few remain today. The kamaburo is a kiln-like domed building covered in a smooth white render, heated by burning spruce. After heating, the embers are removed and wet seaweed or straw mats soaked in seawater are laid on top to create steam. It is said that in 672 AD, Prince Ōama was wounded by an enemy's arrow and bathed in a kamaburo to cure his injury.

The ishiburo is the oldest type of cave sauna common in the area around the Seto Inland Sea. The cave is heated overnight by a fire of green pine and rice straw and then the embers are cleared out and the floor is covered with different seaweeds and medicinal plants such as Japanese mugwort and sweet flag. Straw mats cover the plants and entrance. In the morning the temperature is around 100°C, which cools to around 90°C in the afternoon when villagers gather to bathe and chat. Nearby, a waterfall provides cooling relief. The villagers give thanks for nature's abundance and have built a shrine to the spirits. The ishiburo is valued as a place for relaxation and rejuvenation as well as for alleviating the fatigue of manual labour.

The ishiburo is prepared with water-soaked herbs, citrus fruits and seaweed, before straw mats are laid on top to protect the bathers.
Image © Setouchi Finder

| teamLab & TikTok | teamLab Reconnect: Art with Rinkan Sauna Roppongi | Tokyo, Japan, 2021 |

'Recognising that the mind, body, and environment are the wholeness of our being, we reconnect to the world and time.'

teamLab, 2021

Interdisciplinary art collective teamLab is part of a movement of artists interested in exploring the power of immersive art experiences in unconventional settings, and connecting with audiences outside the realm of traditional gallery-based art. In 2021 teamLab completed TikTok teamLab Reconnect, an extensive sauna and art installation in Tokyo which aims for visitors to experience art in a heightened mental state known as 'sauna trance' or 'totonou'. Research by Yasutaka Kato, Professor of Keio University School of Medicine, has shown that by repeatedly taking hot sauna, cold baths and rest, the bather enters an altered neurological state where the senses sharpen, the mind clears, and the beauty of the surrounding world comes into focus. In this state of totonou, bathers are able to experience artworks more intensely.

The experience includes seven saunas of different temperatures and humidity, each filled with varied music, colour, and scents including white birch, juniper, and hojicha green tea. In the rest area, visitors experience rooms with a series of light-based digital installations that aim to shift perception. Works include *Levitation-Flattening Red and Blue & Violet* in which a light-filled orb floats in the space appearing to defy gravity, and *Proliferating Immense Life in the Rain - A Whole Year per Year,* a huge wall of moving images digitally recreating the lifecycle of flowers in real time as they grow, blossom and decay.

Over the last decade, a growing enthusiasm for sauna in Japan has been influenced in part by manga artist Tanaka Katsuki, who visualised the process of achieving totonou and spread the idea via social media. TeamLab's installation helps to revive the historic practice of Rinkan-Chanoyu. During the Muromachi period (1336–1573) it was popular for a steam bath to be followed by a tea ceremony and art viewing where paintings, hanging scrolls and vases were displayed in the bathing rooms.

Ephemeral Solidified Light, teamLab 2020 at TikTok teamLab Reconnect. The bather walks into a room where they are immersed in a rain of what appear to be solidified light crystals, created by lights refracting in continuous streams of water. Image © teamLab, courtesy Pace Gallery

Massive wood with traditional jointing techniques at the Savusauna Joensuu by Tuomo Siitonen, Asikkala, Finland, 2016.
Image © Rauno Traskelin

5. THE MATERIALS OF SAUNA

Much of the traditional sauna's appeal lies in the elemental experience of raw materials drawn directly from the surrounding forest and suffused in steam.

While wood is the material most immediately associated with the sauna, it is the synergy between wood, stone, earth and water and the transformation of each of these materials through fire and heat that brings the sauna to life.

This primordial experience subconsciously colours our mood and perception of space, and the rich materials in their natural states together create a stimulating and uplifting multi-sensory experience.

There is a growing awareness of the importance of appealing to all the senses – reasserting the value of touch, smell and taste alongside vision and hearing. As Juhani Pallasmaa observes in his essay *The Eyes of the Skin,* architects are 'attempting to re-sensualise architecture' through a strengthened sense of materiality and the haptic, texture and weight, density of space and materialised light. The following material approaches are becoming more prevalent and underlie a growing material philosophy of sauna.

Going forward it is critical that sauna designers take care to consider the provenance of the materials they select and ensure producers adhere to the highest industry standards. Ancient forests in Romania are being devastated by illegal logging, a disaster seen in precious forest ecosystems around the world. The EU estimates that this criminal practice accounts for as much as 40% of the global timber trade. New sauna projects must play their part in the protection and restoration of woodland environments, cherishing wood from forest to sauna and beyond by holding supply chains accountable. Authentic material stories can foster a deeper understanding of culture, place and environment.

Wood

'To enter a wood is to pass into a different world in which we ourselves are transformed.'

Roger Deakin, *Wildwood: A Journey Through Trees*

The smell and texture of raw wood is central to sauna. Both as building material and fuel, it grounds us in natural forces and evokes a more primitive time. Trees are giants of nature, sustaining life with their quiet exchange of carbon dioxide for oxygen. Scientists are only just beginning to understand the complexity of these massive organisms. This awakening to their intelligence coincides with a current cultural interest in trees, seen in the exhibitions 'Trees' at Fondation Cartier and 'Among the Trees' at the Hayward Gallery, in which artists look at the integral relationship between human culture and tree culture. Formafantasma's 'Cambio' at the Serpentine Gallery was an interrogation of the wood industry that highlighted mankind's abuse of this resource that, despite all technological advances, remains central to modern life.

Wood is the most primordial material we use ubiquitously today, and philosopher Emanuele Coccia reminds us that we need a tangible connection with wood in order to feel human. The sauna provides that connection and designers are increasingly aware of how that can be amplified through their approach to wood. Selecting local species will forge a deeper connection to place than using thin slices of industrial timbers. Wood can be worked in a variety of ways, such as charred for longevity or crafted into muscular sculptural forms using digital technologies, opening up new structural possibilities.

Different species of wood are selected for their inherent qualities or symbolic significance. In general, durable softwoods like spruce, red cedar or pine work well for the sauna interior as they absorb heat and don't crack with use. The fragrance emanating from the hot walls should be considered – the examples cited above have distinctive forest smells. To avoid burned bottoms, less dense wood that doesn't become hot to the touch or excrete molten sap is used for benches – aspen works well for this, resinous pine does not. Birch is readily available and used for fuel and whisks.

When used in its natural state, wood appeals to an innate primeval sensibility. It has been proven that close contact with wood brings psychological and physiological benefits such as a reduction in heart rate and an increase in positivity.

Lamune Onsen by Terunobu Fujimori, Oita, Japan, 2005. The structure is clad with cedar treated using the historic Japanese charred-wood process, shou sugi ban. Image © Edmund Sumner-VIEW/Alamy

Clay

Soil gives rise to a location's identity. Its minerals determine which flora grow, and its rich blends offer a ready-made material with which to build. At its most basic, the floor and one or more walls of a primitive sauna were made from earth, as was the adobe of the temazcal and the dugout floor of the sweat lodge. By using this most elemental of materials, saunas harness a connection to the earth's grounding power.

Rammed earth is once again gaining significance around the world as a construction technique that is faithful to place through locally sourced materials and also has a low energy footprint. Historically, earthen buildings are found on every continent. The earliest known are along China's Yellow River and date back to at least 5000 BC. Soil taken directly from the site creates walls that are the colour of the local earth, with small almost decorative colour variations as they are built, layer by layer. If the soil is used in its pure form without any concrete additives, the building can melt back into the earth after serving its purpose. Designers are experimenting with new ways of working with earth, as seen in Mud Frontiers, an experimental project by Rael San Fratello and Emerging Objects, for which a robot was used to 3D-print earth, pointing to a future of highly sophisticated, technical mud construction.

Other vernacular techniques such as cob or adobe can be used to create organic forms. Adobe is formed of earth mixed with water and another material such as straw or dung, sun-baked into bricks. Once built, the walls are covered in an earthen plaster, which may also be painted, producing a smooth, rounded exterior. These low-carbon, low-energy, vernacular techniques exude a simplicity that translates into a feeling of warmth and comfort emanating from the earth.

Liquid mud can also be the bath itself. Rich salinity or minerality from volcanic ash give mud anti-inflammatory and detoxifying properties, meaning that when smothered all over a bather's body, it is both an effective disguise and a wonderful natural therapy.

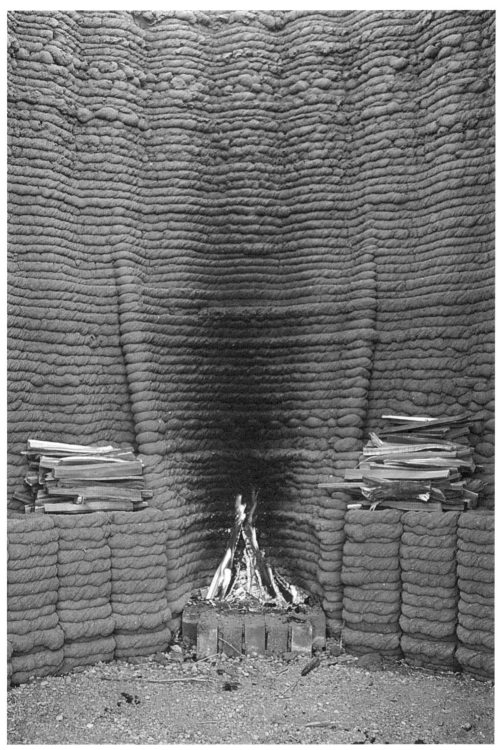

Mud Frontiers by Rael San Fratello and Emerging Objects, San Luis Valley, Colorado, USA, 2019. Image © Emerging Objects

Stone

'Glacial erratics ... granite boulders dropped in place when the glaciers got tired of rolling them. Most of the boulders have been rounded by their journey, but some still stand tall and sharp-edged, like this one ... This elder has sat silently in these lakeshore woods for ten thousand years as forests have come and gone, lake levels ebbed and flowed. ... I come here sometimes just to be in the presence of such ancient beings.'

Robin Wall Kimmerer, *Braiding Sweetgrass*

Stone is the most ancient of materials, spewed from the centre of the earth by volcanoes or formed from the sediment of long disappeared prehistoric seas. In vernacular saunas stone is often used to build the external structure, but all saunas have stones at their heart in the kiuas or stove. Heated to between 500°C and 800°C, the stones used in the fire must *always* be volcanic igneous rocks which have the density and durability that allows for the high heat capacity required for the intensity of sauna. Sedimentary rocks cannot withstand this temperature and are liable to explode dangerously.

There is debate over the best type and shape of stone. Stones should have a surface rough enough to hold water; rounded shapes give a softer löyly while more jagged split-faced stones create a sharper blast of steam. Vulcanite, peridotite, basalt, olivine and granite are all recommended, but in the interest of sauna *terroir* a carefully selected local stone will be most appropriate.

A kiuas, or stove, in a vernacular Finnish savusauna is little more than carefully piled stones with a cavity underneath for the fire. Image © Riku Kettunen

Water

This winter sauna in Ruka, Finland, is constructed with ice blocks that create a humid sauna environment and simply melt back into the lake at the end of the season. Image © Visit Finland / Harri Tarvainen

Water is the least tangible but most crucial material of the sauna. Its magical ability to transition from solid to liquid to almost invisible steam, makes mercurial vapour the symbolic essence of sauna. Liquid water is always present in the sauna for throwing onto the stove where it transforms into the sacred löyly, summoning the spirits. The temperature of a sauna is typically between 75–90°C, but the Finnish Sauna Society, bastion of sauna culture and heritage, has a hot sauna that reaches temperatures over 100°C. In these heats the humidity will be much less than 10%. A cool water source should always be nearby for cleansing and rejuvenating the bather with a cold plunge or a long drink.

Ice is a seasonal component of the sauna. A freezing plunge through an ice hole or a roll in the snow is the most exhilarating contrast to the heat and steam. In winter, igloo-style ice saunas can be built. The purity of ice and the intensity of the heat is cathartic, clearing the mind and boosting energy levels.

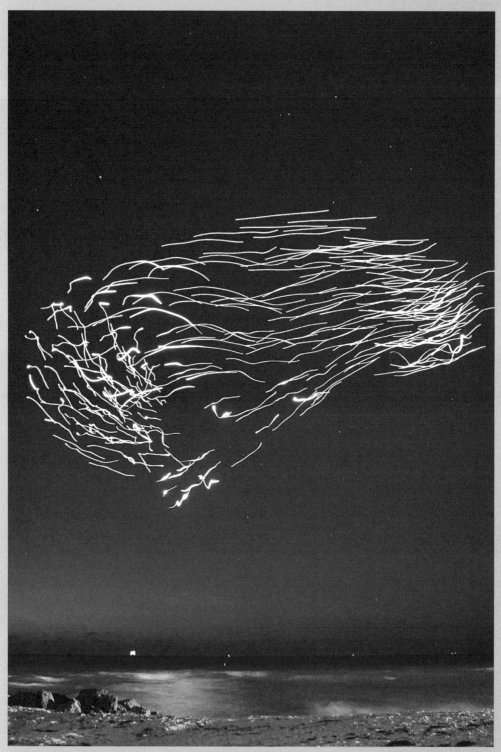

FRANCHISE FREEDOM by DRIFT, Miami, USA, 2017. Image © Jon Ollwerther

6. A THERME VIEW ON BATHING CULTURE

Therme commissioned *Social Sauna* with a view to deepening the understanding of sauna and shaping a contemporary perspective on this ancient bathing culture. Here Jane Withers talked to Stelian Iacob, Therme Group's Senior Vice President, about sauna and city life, art and wellbeing.

Interview with Stelian Iacob,
Senior Vice President at Therme Group

Jane Withers   I'm interested to learn more about Therme's ambition for the sauna and why you consider the experience so important for setting the future course for the Therme resorts?

Stelian Iacob   Sauna culture, in its broadest sense, is profoundly aligned with Therme's values which promote a holistic approach to wellbeing. This idea of preventative healthcare, a better lifestyle and habits.

   Sauna is also a wonderful means to promote the sort of social gathering and communal spirit that we want to have within our resorts. To make a place where everybody meets on equal ground without the constraints of society, without clothes, without pressure.

JW   I think this spirit of communality is fundamental to the revival of interest in sauna in the last few years. My understanding is that Therme is really honing its focus on wellbeing and a contemporary wellbeing culture. How do you see sauna fitting into that?

SI   Well, I think sauna is a wonderful tool for bettering people's lives because it is a ritual as much as it is a practice and a healthy habit. We need to think of wellbeing in a holistic way. As we see through your research, sauna has physical and mental health benefits, nurtures awareness, and alongside that you have food, and culture too. One of the problems with Western societies is that we are embedded in an empirical approach – people are only convinced of the benefits of sauna if you have the data and research about it. Although sauna research is quite extensive, it's never enough because people want to have absolute proof of its benefits.

   Instead, we propose that through research and the arts, we can better understand sauna culture, its roots and how rituals originated and grew into people's subconscious. Using these learnings, we can take the Therme experience and introduce new healthy rituals to the world with a truly global perspective, from North America all the way to Asia, to incorporate that link between a local bathing culture and wellbeing.

JW   What you are saying is fascinating. That we have become frightened of a qualitative experience, or lost the tools or trust in ourselves to evaluate it. Therme's vision opens the space for people to understand for themselves. How will the research on sauna be reflected in the next phase of Therme's development?

FRANCHISE FREEDOM by DRIFT at Burning Man, Black Rock Desert, USA, September 2018. Image © Rahi Rezvani

SI   Part of the Therme concept is to have wellbeing intertwined with all the activities, with a big emphasis on sauna and heat therapies. We would like to be as authentic as possible because the experience is as much emotional and spiritual as it is physical. You can't have the technological part alone, that needs to be almost magic and disappear, but you need to promote the authenticity and the real feeling of sauna bathing. This is done only by understanding the culture and spirit, and what it means for different cultures around the world.

JW   In the Therme resorts of the future, will we see more focus given to the depth of the sauna experience?

SI   That's the idea. We also want to reimagine the sauna experience in new ways. The idea being that, first of all, you take the ideas of grounding, of access and connection of people to earth and the elements, and at the same time, we create new ways of experiencing saunas that can take you into new dimensions. Through architecture, and through art integrated in the sauna experience. The Therme experience is a personal journey towards reconnecting with your wellbeing, with yourself.

JW   And how design and architecture could holistically help generate this experience is a fascinating field for exploration. So much of our architecture is a visual culture and we forget what it's actually like to experience these places through temperature, through touch, through all the senses. More generally, how do you see wellbeing culture evolving in the next decade and how will this be reflected in future Therme resorts?

SI   Wellbeing is more present in people's minds recently due to the unprecedented times and the pandemic exaggerating a lot of global issues. At the same time, a desire to live a better life is embedded in our human nature and that drives this renewed wellbeing culture. In the modern era we have lost our connection to nature and to healthy practices. As we begin to understand the importance of that, we try to reconnect through different tools and mediums, reconnect to the earth, to nature and ecosystems. Wellbeing in the future cannot be separated from that. Through reconnection with nature, we can rediscover our internal wellbeing. In the future, we aim to have Therme wellbeing resorts in the city centre to achieve the aim of improving people's health by being accessible, by being central, and easy to make part of your daily routine.

JW   In 2020, Therme Art developed the Wellbeing Culture Forum as a proactive response to the pandemic and global crisis. After the past year we're all much more open to change and aware of the importance of wellbeing on a personal and societal level. What are the learnings at Therme Group from this series of far-reaching and diverse debates?

SI   This all started with the green paper that Therme Group commissioned, 'Human Cities', where we asked what will wellbeing mean in the cities of tomorrow. We try to understand how those of us living in modern cities can access wellbeing as part of normal lives. A lot of questions arose from that paper. For example, is the wellbeing of their citizens something that cities actively pursue and is it in the interests of cities to pursue? We created the Wellbeing Culture Forum to deepen the understanding and bring together different perspectives on the same subject. The speakers presented many teachings and simple, considerate things that you can do to improve people's lives. That has been really extraordinary.

JW   A fantastic avenue to open up, particularly this year. What struck me was that you were doing so much of your thinking in public, in an open, generous way. And I think that's where it really gains momentum. Can you tell me more about how you see Therme Art manifesting in the resorts in future?

SI   Therme Art is a wonderful initiative that speaks to our community and is embedded in social engagement and access. We wanted to explore how to integrate and commission art within Therme resorts. Art is an intrinsic part of our wellbeing and an essence of our societal struggles, our personal conflicts. Today the arts are compartmental-ised by discipline, and separated from daily life, but we believe this isn't a good idea. People in Roman times did not make a distinction between the arts, they were merged for the benefit of people.

One of the first Therme Art projects was FRANCHISE FREEDOM by DRIFT, a mesmerising sculpture of up to 600 drones, each a light source in the night sky, whose flying movements mimic the murmuration of starlings, uniting audiences, technology and nature.

The project was first presented by DRIFT to coincide with their 'Coded Nature' exhibition at the Stedelijk Museum in Amsterdam. Therme Art and Pace have since joined forces with the artists to support the long-term development and touring of the performative artwork, which has now been presented at Burning Man 2018, NASA's Kennedy Space Center 2019, Al Ula 2020, and as a surprise performance in Rotterdam as a symbol of hope amid the global pandemic. And that's only the beginning, we will have so much more art integrated within Therme.

Serpentine Pavilion 2021 by Counterspace, directed by Sumayya Vally and purchased by Therme Art. Based on Vally's research into community meeting places across London, the pavilion's design explores themes of identity and belonging.
Image © Iwan Baan

The Mother by Egill Sæbjörnsson, digital drawing, 2019

Therme Art was founded in 2017 with the aim of amplifying the way that we engage with art in our everyday lives by enabling both internationally recognised artists and architects, and new talents to realise site-specific projects outside the gallery context and in Therme's resorts. The far-reaching vision of Mikolaj Sekutowicz has quickly developed a significant artistic and cultural programme. His belief that artists and architects can transform urban environments to support people's wellbeing is the result of an open and heterogeneous approach that embraces ideas of global thinkers including scientists, philosophers and shamans.

'Therme Art believes that through the ideas and creativity of artists, cities and urban development can be re-shaped to meet the physical and spiritual needs of humans, allowing us to reconnect with our inner selves.'

Mikolaj Sekutowicz, CEO and Curator of Therme Art

Therme Art has developed partnerships with leading institutions including the Serpentine Gallery, Manchester International Festival and Design Miami. Since 2018, Therme Art has supported the annual Serpentine Pavilion, London, most recently by emerging architects Counterspace (page 99).

Therme Art is continually looking to work with the most forward-thinking forces in art, design, science and city planning. One of these is Superblue, a new initiative for experiential and immersive art. Working alongside Superblue, Therme Art is supporting artists to realise ambitious visions, while also helping global audiences to experience the wellbeing benefits of art.

In the longer term, Therme Art will embed art within Therme resorts through a series of ambitious commissions that allow artists to realise projects that they could not achieve without its support. These commissions aim to transform the visitor experience by bringing art to audiences who might not otherwise encounter creativity in their daily lives.

'It is within these conceptual spaces that we can explore new ways of thinking beyond our current limitations, allowing us to imagine and generate ways of programming cities that are more creative, sustainable and free'

Mikolaj Sekutowicz

Wellbeing Culture Forum

In response to the unfolding global pandemic of 2020 which brought the deficiencies of our urban environments and ways of living into sharp focus, Therme Art initiated the Wellbeing Culture Forum to explore links between art, environment, nature and wellbeing. Reflecting on what is needed to restore bodies and minds following months of lockdown, luminaries from art, design and science come together to explore how creativity might address these issues and envision the future of wellbeing and healthy cities.

To date the Forum has addressed a number of themes including community-led design, re-designing rituals, the role of wellbeing in architecture and city planning, and the relevance of the Gaia Hypothesis today. A digital-physical incarnation of the forum took place in the König Galerie, Berlin in September 2020 and interspersed discussions on 'From Breaking Bauhaus to Growing Gaia' with art commissions and food experiences.

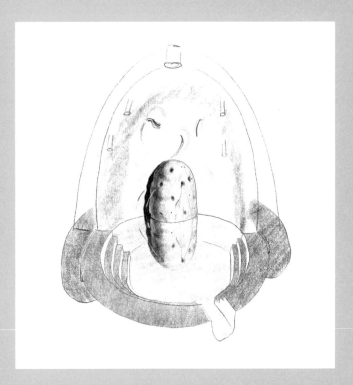

The Mother

The first Therme Art commission by Icelandic artist Egill Sæbjörnsson will be installed at a Therme Group facility. Berlin-based Sæbjörnsson is a multimedia artist and musician whose work explores the connections between our thoughts and what is happening in the world around us. He has been working with self-generated projections since 2012, where the image source is programmed to infinitely produce images, experimenting with technology as a continuation of his drawings and paintings, and a means to explore the relationship between humans and the environment in a playful way. Sæbjörnsson was nominated for a Carnegie Art Award in 2010 and represented Iceland at the 57th Venice Biennale of Art in 2017.

    The Mother takes the form of a 15-metre dome by a lake which visitors reach via a series of walkways and enter by immersing themselves in the water and travelling through an entrance lagoon to the dome's centre. The installation is envisaged as a journey for the senses, inspired by the egalitarian ethos of Roman baths. Inside, visitors will encounter an amphitheatre with a fountain at its centre where they can take time to reflect. Water is at the heart of the artwork, experienced both physically, and through digital projections of flying water which allow this mysterious element to travel in ways that are not physically possible, underlining the otherworldly magic of this essential element.

The Mother
by Egill Sæbjörnsson,
digital drawing, 2019

The Forest Project by Saaren Kartano and Viivi Roiha with photographer Isla Peura, brings circus arts to the forest.
Image © Isla Peura

8. WELLBEING

Traditionally, sauna offers a contrasting tempo, a deep connection to nature and a sense of community. Experimental sauna culture builds on this age-old practice, uniting scientific understanding and ancient knowledge with experimental forms of cultural expression, branching out into related areas such as ritual, performance, exercise and food. These new areas create opportunities for embodied learning that re-establish a visceral connection to the natural world and help to develop a profound sense of reciprocity with the environment. Here, we explore some of the key themes of this wellbeing ethos and the creatives working in this area, including shamans, herbalists, artists and performers.

Mind and Body

The current renewed interest in sauna, as with practices such as mindfulness, meditation and yoga, reflects sauna's commonly reported ability to mitigate stress, anxiety and other mental health issues that are exacerbated in the contemporary world by relentless digital connectivity and smartphone addiction. New anxieties resulting from the Covid-19 pandemic present further challenges that are yet to be fully recognised and understood.

Yale Medical Center research has found 'stress-related illnesses result in the highest global disease burden worldwide'. Acknowledging the symbiotic relationship between mind and body is at the heart of a growing shift in the medical establishment's focus away from methods of diagnosis and treatment, towards understanding how healthy lifestyles and wellness can prevent illness in the first place.

A review of existing research published by the Mayo Clinic lists physical and therapeutic benefits that sauna and bathing rituals have to offer. These include a reduction in risk of cardiovascular and neurodegenerative disease, better immune responses and improved sleep. By providing a profound interaction with the natural world, sauna can additionally counteract the symptoms of Nature Deficit Disorder, enhancing mental acuity and creativity.

Woodcut from the title page of *The Grete Herball*, 1526

Forest Apothecary

As this research has shown, sauna practices have an abiding link to the forest and to wood in both an imaginative and material sense. The influential environmental psychologists Rachel and Stephen Kaplan's landmark research established the many advantages spending time in nature can bring to human health in the late 1980s. The recent resurgence of interest in trees and wood stems from the realisation that forests are critical to healthy ecosystems, as well as from the recognition that there is extraordinary value in the knowledge that we can re-learn from lost forest wisdom.

Nature Deficit Disorder has become an identifiable phenomenon and is symptomatic of ignoring our inescapable and enduring reliance on the natural environment for holistic wellbeing. The Japanese practice of shinrin-yoku, or forest bathing, is the impetus behind the establishment of Forest Medicine as a field of scientific research that is seeking to establish ways of re-integrating a forest connection into nature-starved urban lives. The research of immunologist and Forest Medicine expert Dr Qing Li has found that it is the scent of a forest, specifically that of the oils emitted by trees, that has the most beneficial effect on forest bathers. The smell of arboreal phytoncides has been shown to lift depression and anxiety, decrease stress hormones and boost the production of anti-cancer proteins.

As well as a guide to understanding the forest as a living apothecary, folklore traditions around the world suggest ways of tapping into less tangible forest powers. Since time immemorial humans have used rituals and ceremonies to evoke the spirits of the woodland and forge a deep connection to the sacred energy of the forest. We need to re-invent these practices to fulfil the same ancient need in the present day.

Atmosphere: Sound and Smell

One of the benefits of sauna is the opening up to a full sensory experience. The physiological, neurological and psychological potential of sound, smell and resonance is vast; studies of the visual effects of nature have tended to dominate research but, as reviewed in the *International Journal of Environmental Research and Public Health* the possibilities for affecting health and wellbeing via the less dominant senses are beginning to be understood.

Sound has the potential to create a profoundly poetic resonance of space. The practice of sound bathing uses resonant notes created by singing bowls, gongs or even the human voice to help participants access a meditative state. Lukas Kühne's sound installation at Tvísöngur in Iceland uses an architectural structure to achieve a similar effect. Each dome has a resonance that corresponds to a tone in the Icelandic musical tradition of five-tone harmony, working as a natural amplifier. Visitors can play with the ethereal acoustics in the remote setting. Similarly, at Therme Vals, architect Peter Zumthor designed a sound pool or resonance room which amplifies the voices of the users to create an immersive sound experience.

Full-body immersion, whether in the medium of steam, water or sound, can have an exhilarating and potentially transcendental effect. Introducing new bathing mediums into the ritual can stimulate body and mind in new ways.

Tvísöngur by Lukas Kühne, Seyðisfjörður, Iceland. Images © Lukas Kühne/Gudmundur Oddur Magnússon and Paul Theophil Haegi

Sissel Tolaas collecting a tree smell. Image © Sissel Tolaas / Timothy Seppala

The smell of wood, smoke and herbs is an important part of a traditional sauna experience which could be reimagined. Like sound, smell also has the ability to create a subtle, yet powerful, connection to nature, as seen in the work of artist Sissel Tolaas, who has previously collaborated with Therme Art. Tolaas created a forest scent for Formafantasma's 'Cambio' exhibition which explored the wood industry at the Serpentine, setting the scene for visitors as they arrived in the gallery. Her work is also evidence of how smell can connect with the subconscious, evoking powerful emotions and memories which are fundamental in the development of environmental empathy.

Another example is *Foris*, a 2018 work presented at Unsound Festival Krakow by field-recording artist and Therme Art collaborator Chris Watson, perfumer Geza Schön and lighting artist Marcel Weber, which conjures the atmosphere of a forest environment. This immersive installation combines a multi-layered forest smellscape with recordings from seven endangered forest ecosystems around the world. Drenching all the senses is a way of transporting the mind as well as the body and can add a powerful extra dimension to the sauna experience.

Ritual and Performance

Driftwood City by Anna
Halprin at Experiments in
Environment Workshop, Sea
Ranch CA, USA, July 4, 1966

Wherever and whenever a sauna takes place, ritual is always key to the experience. Creating the löyly, the alternation of hot steam and cold plunge, cooling off and drinking beer with friends afterwards. Design, materiality and atmosphere all contribute to the creation of an environment that heightens the potential for ritual, and helps establish a rhythm to the practice of sauna bathing that can develop embodied knowledge of its culture and principles.

Performance is a central component of ritual, a process that, like sauna, allows a participant to inhabit an alternative space removed from the everyday. In *The Logic of Practice* Pierre Bourdieu wrote that 'the body believes in what it plays at' and physically embodying expressions of healing, environmental awareness or mindfulness is an effective way of establishing radical new forms of understanding and empathy. This process is expressed in the work of choreographer Anna Halprin. A pioneer of the expressive arts healing movement, for many years Halprin's work has explored ways of healing the body and community through movement and dance. In the late 1960s, Halprin and her husband Lawrence organised a series of experimental, cross-disciplinary workshops along the coast of California that brought together dancers, architects, designers and artists to explore new approaches to environmental awareness.

Her work Planetary Dance, created to restore peace and health to the planet, has become a midsummer rite performed across the world. Recent performances at MoMA PS1 and documenta 14 are part of a current revival of interest in Halprin's work, and recognise anew the potential for communicating important ideas through performative movement and ritual.

As well as staging lectures and exhibitions about sauna culture and providing instructions for anyone wishing to build their own, the Bauhaus Sauna Society use traditional sauna as the starting point to develop new rituals, combining them with Walter Gropius's original Bauhaus vision to bring together artists and craftsmen from different disciplines to create a better world. Like Halprin, they look beyond the boundaries of conventional performance, engaging with the world around them through ritualised movement to explore better ways of being. This approach opens up endless possibilities for new rituals informed by specific place, time and individual need.

Ritual created by the Bauhaus Sauna Society photographed during 'Expedition Exhibition – defining the 21st century explorer', Kemijärvi, Finland, June 2011. Image © Alexander Lembke

Shamanism, Purification and Metamorphosis

The feeling of emerging from a sauna is one of being transformed. As has already been noted, this sensation has long been harnessed by Northern shamans, for whom 'the sauna is where all the transitions happen'. For Indigenous American shamans the sweat lodge is similarly central to sacred rituals of prayer and purification that use the consciousness-altering effects of the heat and steam to bring about a new spiritual awareness.

Just like sauna, shamanism uses ritual to enable participants 'to enter non-ordinary reality', chiefly for problem solving and healing. Practices like repetitive drumming can be used to achieve an altered state, although some shamanic rituals include the consumption of psychoactive plants such as ayahuasca to intensify the process. Contemporary shamanism, as practised by the late Dr Michael Harner and his Foundation for Shamanic Studies, California, teaches knowledge and techniques that combine ancient wisdom with modern science and Western ethics. Shamanistic methods can inform the development of new sauna rituals and point to possibilities for applying these practices to contemporary life with a focus on enhancing creativity, forging connections with the environment and enacting positive change.

Seasonality

A traditional sauna bathing experience is directly shaped by the seasons – experienced in the smells and sensations of fresh herbs or dried birch leaves, a chilly plunge through the ice or a refreshing jump into a sun-warmed lake. Winding down might take place outside on sun-lit summer evenings or in flickering firelight in winter. Allowing seasonal changes to inform the sauna bathing experience creates changing rhythms to the rituals and forges a direct connection with the place and the passing of time. While the sauna is important for warmth during the hard winter, it is also at the centre of Finnish midsummer celebrations, known as Juhannus. In addition to sauna bathing, this is a time when bonfires are lit, birch leaves are made into fresh sauna whisks, wildflowers are gathered and spells are cast for good fortune in the year ahead.

Food

Eating and drinking something as you wind down from a sauna bath is an important aspect of the ritual, helping the body regain equilibrium and providing an opportunity to commune with fellow bathers. Traditional sauna foods are Nordic specialities drawn from the forest and lake such as smoked meat and fish, sometimes smoked in the same sauna in which the bathing takes place. Feasts for special festivals would include seasonal delicacies such as foraged berries and wild mushrooms picked in the surrounding forest.

Fundamental to wellbeing and closely linked with the same holistic spirit, sauna and food cultures are underpinned by many shared principles. Both have been influenced by the current return to localism and the revival of traditional cultures that have evolved to fulfil contemporary needs. 'The New Nordic Food Manifesto' is a call from leading chefs of the region to develop an innovative approach to traditional cuisine, combined with a strong focus on health and ethical production. As well as considering food as part of the sauna offering, sauna can take a lead from the ethos of progressive food cultures that are establishing new authenticities and ecologically-sound models for living well.

The Copenhagen restaurant Noma has pushed the boundaries of New Nordic cuisine with a hyperlocal and micro-seasonal menu. Many of the vegetables and herbs they serve are foraged from the woods and countryside around the city. Image © Noma

Food as Medicine

Food is central to self-care and nutrition, and can be the safest remedy for many common health problems. Like many other physical activities, it also has a direct impact on mental health. Living Medicine is an organisation that teaches and promotes the use of food and herbs for health and wellbeing at a community level and works to establish a close relationship between growing and eating. As Alex Laird of Living Medicine has said, 'When we are feeding the body through the mouth, we are also feeding the mind.'

The food designer Marije Vogelzang takes a light-hearted approach to the understanding of food as medicine in her many explorations of how food affects the body. She has created menus designed to wake you up or calm you down, and uses different coloured foods to incite different moods and emotions. Food and sauna are just two means of influencing wellbeing but, as Vogelzang shows, there is scope for exploring fresh approaches. Designers are increasingly experimenting with unusual combinations of food and esoteric therapeutic practices, often creative interpretations of ancient ideas.

Chef Antto Melasniemi at Sompasauna, Helsinki, Finland. Image © Emilia Kangasluoma

Food as Culture

Food is simultaneously 'nature, technology and culture', and as such has tremendous potential for going beyond nutrition to become performance and ritual. The Serpentine Gallery's 'Radical Kitchen' programme in 2017 has incorporated food, art and performance into a series of events that is a key reference for a creative engagement with food and its role in living cultures.

The Finnish chef Antto Melasniemi is a food visionary, musician, performer and sauna lover. He combines his knowledge of traditional Finnish cuisine with other contemporary cultures from around the world and his own unique performative vision. A recent project is *The Bastard Cookbook,* created with Thai artist Rirkrit Tiravanija. This collection of recipes is 'an exploration of comradery, improvisation, and cosmopolitanism' that 'eschew[s] the sanctity of tradition' for an imaginative, bastardised style of cooking that draws upon the two men's personal multi-cultural history. As Melasniemi points out, when it comes to food, 'authenticity is absurd'. Melasniemi has said that for him 'music and food are two different ways of telling a story'. Thinking about sauna as storytelling and being, like Melasniemi, open to a melting pot of influences opens up a rich world of possibility for creating new wellbeing narratives that foreground the values and potential for sauna discussed here.

Excerpts from 'The New Nordic Food Manifesto'

→   Be an expression of purity, simplicity and ethical production.

→   Reflect the different seasons.

→   Work with quality raw materials specific to place and time.

→   Combine good taste with modern knowledge about health and wellbeing.

→   Sensitively combine the best local traditions with modern impulses from elsewhere.

One Man Sauna by modulorbeat, Bochum, Germany, 2014. Image © Jan Kampshoff/modulorbeat

9. SOCIAL SAUNA — A NEW PERSPECTIVE

During this extensive exploration of the world of sauna, we have seen many approaches to the practice, from the deliberate and careful conservation of the vernacular, to the playful spirit of ad hoc saunas and breathtaking contemporary spaces. Sauna culture embodies so much of what it is to be human, a ritual honed by generations of instinct, embodied knowledge and experience married with curiosity and invention.

Looking to the future, we consider that the significance of sauna lies not in blindly following traditional practices, but in understanding sauna's essence and defining new approaches to wellbeing. It is this holistic perspective, alongside a growing sense of community and environmental consciousness, that is driving sauna's renewed following. At the same time, bathing entrepreneurs are increasingly engaging with practitioners at the forefront of contemporary thinking – from architects to neuroscientists, from nutritionists to performance artists – to enhance the sauna experience. This progressive, trans-disciplinary approach is developing imaginative and effective responses to the many stresses we face, from an individual to a societal level.

Here we summarise some of the key learnings from our research that we consider influential in shaping a new sauna culture:

→ Sauna is a transformative ritual that can take us out of our transactional daily lives. In new sauna cultures practitioners are working with artists, herbalists and performers among others to develop rituals that re-establish a visceral connection to the real in the face of the increasing dominance of the digital and rising levels of anxiety associated with it.

→ The sauna is a powerful tool for building community, comradery, and connection with others, and there is a growing momentum towards this, through the creation of events, rituals, performances and installations that bring people together.

→ New sauna spaces are acknowledging the importance of the haptic to the metamorphic power of sauna. Understanding the possibilities of sensory engagement can enhance sauna's potential to support psychological wellbeing. Through further research in neuroarchitecture, new sauna designs can foster a growing understanding of how the body and brain respond to the environment and can tap into embodied knowledge.

→ Natural materials in raw and massive states are at the heart of the sauna experience. Sauna designers should adopt a more conscious approach to sourcing and construction that integrates a better understanding of sustainability and circularity.

→ There is a trend for saunas to foreground exposure to the wild and elemental as a restorative therapy that can help counter conditions such as Nature Deficit Disorder. Establishing a meaningful connection to nature is part of fostering environmental awareness.

→ Until comparatively recently, the vast majority of humans had a deep indigenous understanding of the environment in which they lived: its flora, fauna and topography. As has been discussed throughout this paper, there is much to be gained by re-engaging with the biotope of a specific place. Innovative sauna practices take reference from local heritage, materials, water, food, minerals and herbs, fostering a deep connection to place.

→ As discussed in Ritual and Performance, directly experiencing new knowledge, whether through a performed ritual or a full-body sensory interaction, can lead to profound embodied understanding. Sauna practitioners are developing methods for learning in this experiential way. At the same time there is renewed interest in the sauna as a cultural space.

→ The sauna journey is a powerful tool to revive interest in water therapies and deepen our connection to seasonality and water culture.

CREDITS & RESOURCES

Content and Editors:
Jane Withers and Ria Hawthorn
Jane Withers Studio

Wellbeing:
Miranda Vane, Jane Withers Studio

Jane Withers is a leading design consultant, curator and writer. Her London-based studio works with cultural institutions and brands to shape design-led strategies and programmes that bring innovative design thinking to address societal and environmental challenges.

Jane has curated critically acclaimed exhibitions and publications for the Victoria and Albert Museum and the Royal Academy of Arts among many others. She teaches and speaks internationally and has served on numerous juries and advisory boards. Jane has long had a special interest in water and bathing culture and has extensive experience of engaging creatively with the issues surrounding water sustainability. *www.janewithers.com*

Commissioned by Therme Group
Therme Group is a leading global wellbeing provider designing, constructing, and operating the world's largest wellbeing facilities. Its contemporary urban development proposition incorporates environmental concepts to re-integrate nature into everyday life. Therme Group's facilities combine its innovative sustainable technologies with human-oriented design. Drawing upon the tradition of ancient thermal baths, which were designed to be healing, social, and egalitarian settings, Therme Group builds environments that nurture the mind and body for visitors of all ages and demographics, creating healthy and resilient communities. *www.thermegroup.com*

Project Manager
Elena Morariu

Graphic Design & Art Direction
Sarah Boris

Layout
Andrei Ion

Sub-editor
Alison Hissey

Acknowledgements:
Thanks to the following for their valuable insight to sauna culture:
Kimmo Raitio
Lassi A. Liikkanen
Mika Meskanen, British Sauna Society
Sami Rintala, Rintala Eggertsson

Additional photographic credits

All images are reproduced with the permission of the copyright holder. Every effort has been made to trace the photographers of the images. Additional credits are as follows:

Further Reading & Resources

Aaland, Mikkel, *Sweat* (Capra Press, 1978)

Aaland, Mikkel, *Perfect Sweat* series (2017 – ongoing)
www.perfectsweatseries.com

Bakolis, I. et al. 'Urban Mind: Using Smartphone Technologies to Investigate the impact of Nature on Mental Wellbeing in Real Time', *BioScience*, 68(2), Feb 2018, 134–145

Berghall, Joonas & Hotakainen, Mika (dir.), *Steam of Life,* 2011

Bourdieu, Pierre, *The Logic of Practice* (Stanford University Press, 1990)

Cohen, Marc, 'Turning up the heat on COVID-19: heat as a therapeutic intervention', *F1000Res,* July 2020

Deakin, Roger, *Wildwood: A Journey Through Trees* (Hamish Hamilton, 2007)

Franco, Lara S. et al. 'A Review of the Benefits of Nature Experiences: More Than Meets the Eye' in *International Journal of Environmental Research and Public Health* 2017, August 14 (8) 864

International Arts and Mind Lab blog
www.artsandmindlab.org/blog

International Smoke Sauna Society
savusauna.fi

Kaldera, Raven, *Wightridden: Paths of Northern-Tradition Shamanism* (Asphodel Press, 2007)

Kaplan, Rachel & Stephen, *The Experience of Nature: A Psychological Perspective* (Cambridge University Press, 1989)

Kaskinen, Teijo, *Sauna – The Essence of Finland* (Kirjakaari, 2011)

Koren, Leonard, *Undesigning the Bath* (Stonebridge Press, 1996)

Laird, Alex 'An Introduction to Living Medicine'
www.livingmedicine.org

Laukkanen, J. A. et al. 'Cardiovascular and Other Health Benefits of Sauna Bathing: A Review of the Evidence' in *Mayo Clinic Proceedings* 2018;93(8):1111-1121

Li, Qing, *Forest Bathing: How Trees Can Help You Find Health and Happiness* (Penguin Random House, 2018)

Martin, Leanne, 'Nature contact, nature connectedness and associations with health, wellbeing and environmental behaviours', *Journal of Environmental Psychology,* April 2020

Melasniemi, Antto & Tiravanija, Rirkrit, *The Bastard Cookbook* (Garret Publications, 2019)

Meyer, Claus et al. *New Nordic Kitchen Manifesto,* 2004

Pallasmaa, Juhani, *The Eyes of the Skin: Architecture and the Senses* (John Wiley and Sons, 2005)

Pelo, June, *The Sauna,* Swedish Finn Historical Society
www.swedishfinnhistoricalsociety.org/the-sauna

raumlabor, 'Goteborg Bathing Culture', *Domus,* 20 October 2015

Sang-Hun, Chloe, 'Kiln Saunas Make a Comeback in South Korea', *New York Times,* 26 August 2010

The Foundation for Shamanic Studies
www.shamanism.org

Toivonen, Tuomas, 'Ten Commandments of the Public Bath', *Well, Well, Well (Harvard Design Magazine),* no. 40, S/S 2015

Vogelzang, Marije
https://www.marijevogelzang.nl/

Wall Kimmerer, Robin, *Braiding Sweetgrass: Indigenous Wisdom, Scientific Knowledge and the Teachings of Plants* (Penguin, 2020)

Watson, Julia, *Lo—TEK, Design by Radical Indigenism* (Taschen, 2019)

Welsh Government Technical Advisory Group 'Swimming Pools, Hot Tubs, Saunas and Steam Rooms and Risk from Covid-19', 4 November 2020

Wohlleben, Peter, *The Hidden Life of Trees: What They Feel, How They Communicate, Discoveries from a Secret World* (Greystone Books, 2015)